Penny Ante Feud 16
Poor Bird

Shoe
Music
Press

Benjamin Schmitt

Broken marriage

Spider webs hang like veils
over the dying summer breeze
tear down the state
of being
that is teatotaling
in a bear costume
on an unknown riverbank
the cows gather by the fence post
I have no more lies to tell you
they don't pay me for that anymore
pastures are swept aside
by the force of my connubial tongue
protestors are sleeping in a park
because there is no place else to gather
an occupying force
they have invaded their own town
I have lost my way
inside a series of wild minutes
surrounded by
the clenched fists of days
I occupied the bank until I had no more money
it is cold and wet
the world is crowded
they make us feel so safe
when we hand them our credit cards
after walking through the deforestation of time
I came upon a ranch surrounded by marble sculptures
an abused woman lived here
but she would not leave with me

even after he broke her bones upon the floor
she was an occupant in a marriage
this is not the same as a wife

Zach Knox

Edict of books on tape:

life,
a flawless mistake
squandered god given gifts
disposed of
in strumming percussion and humming bass lines
felt in the air tonight
raises eyebrow concern
stark, starving
self in poor mental health
alienates the lifelong grift of societies promised wealth
cured by beer;
a given advice
to be a lover
One should know how
to fight or write.

the moment You walked through
the door
i renounced all nouns
i'd known before

You moved across
the room
like the flick of a cigarette
cool and hot
heaven or hell
sent

generous with greed
few years younger than
me.
to leave
to stay
fascinate me
in a blurring
bookmark back to this night/day
reliving this hangover
with each turn of a

punch clock page.

Shannon Jackson

Poor Bird

what if your help crippled
what if you set nothing free

everything you ever needed
didn't need you

I sewed his wings to his body
I broke his beak and glued the shards together
I spoon fed him lies like worms through his shattered throat
I lie on my stomach, like the snake I am, and I ache for him

   poor bird, poor bird

we're in this together;
   don't worry,
I'll never leave you

JD DeHart

Lapping

Even the dogs have water
to drink, and even the lower
animals have refreshments.
The rodents have nicer sweaters
than the ones we are sporting.
It makes me full of sorrow to see
the picks and holes in your fine
clothing, reminding me of a junior
high music teacher, struggling
to make ends meet,
how we made her cry one day,
the cassette tape still crooning.
The empty plates are eyes
watching me, waiting to see
the choices I will make now.

BZ Niditch

Toxicity City

A grassy lover's lane
on any country field
in Toxicity City
can contain
consequences,
I told a guy at my gig
who asked me
where such love is
around here.
I told him
such love
may be off the beaten track
or in unfriendly woods
where there are ticks
in the midst
of a July heat wave
or by the Cape's shore
on wet blankets.
I encouraged him to stay away
from the fields of poison ivy
and the dangerous traffic
on the muddy roads
but he was so needy
for any highway love
and being a dare devil
made his moves
when he met his soul mate
that night at a jazz club
but by the next week

he had cooled off
she had already left him
a hundred miles away.

Sal Marici

Stuck After Six Hours of Socializing

His Brit accent begins to slip
like suds on the sides
in his empty glass.
He lives in England
but this week he visits
Iowa, his home state,
talking soccer stats.
He calls us mates

as I sit on his mother's porch
with four others in Le Claire.
We overlook Cody Street
and the Mississippi
after Tug Fest fireworks
before burnt air disperses.
Cars roll   stop
motorcycles rev   cough
when the light a mile from us
turns green   red.

I shift, face the Englishman
ask a question
to show I have not left
then resume my position
watch for thinned traffic
while their longhair tabby
sits on my lap. I pet.
She sniffs my cat's scent.

Later the tabby curls on a chair.
"*Of course*," she says to herself.
"*Of course, they want to be alone.*
I would too."
The thirteen-pound orange body
wrapped in white stripes stands.
Front legs stretch across the seat.
Paw bats catnip mouse to floor.

"*Of course, they want to be alone.*" and "'*Of course,' she said to herself.*" are lines from *Red Pony* by John Steinbeck

June Sylvester Saraceno

United This

belly dancers turn burlesque
        duck lips and
                bushy browns plucked into
                    a winged frown

hoedowns turn electric
        flags sown onto underpants wax patriotic

the jade vase fires back from a pedestal
        don't push me cuz I'm close to the edge

        orthodox hipsters hopscotch
        with fanatics in babushkas
        on a sidewalk neither owns
           where at night the pops are loud
        louder still the quiet after

cowboys claim it

        the police claim it

                the government claims it

                    apple pie and baseball claim it

                    Baptists claim it

                        factory girl claims it

maybe it's up for grabs
maybe its districts redraw themselves
maybe it's ripe for the plucking, for the picking
finger lickin'
refried
homogenized
resegregated
orchestrated co-opting of cultural cherry blossom
blues-thumpin', head bumpin'
spaghetti western of home spun violence

it's noir   it's not

it's a robbery taking place every second

Anne Lovering Rounds

Orpheus epilogue

Orpheus had it figured out:
we're always losing each other
by accident, looking back
or pressing too hard and

what will mitigate but not reverse this loss
is a sequence in the third movement
of the Italian Concerto I didn't even
remember was there until it happened

Ian C. Smith

Happiness

I buried valuables in the ticking bush
above a dry gully where we wallowed in angry misery
on my father's latest failure, a chicken farm;
tobacco, a girl's address, cash stolen in increments
from a shop on weekends where I worked hard
after enduring school every brutal week.

Also dormant like them, film-noir inspired,
were fanciful hopes I nursed, planned to disinter
when I turned fourteen, school-leaving age.
My boss, king of contempt, sneered at my sweated shirt
unaware of white-collar crime,
the takings always tallying at day's end.

A mopoke observed me claim this meagre stake,
my chained dog barking to a pockmarked moon.
After hitching to our end-of-the-line station
I rode the last train that night, a smell of steel,
squares of light, the image of a boy's face,
inventing his story ahead, happiness.

Joseph Saling

Everlast

I) The Negative

This piece of film was stuck inside a book,
And there, preserved from dust and hands, it saved
The image of a boy and man who looks
Too young to be the father in the grave.

The years between these silhouettes and you
Feel like a dream that fades by day. I have
No memory of prints like this. The two
Of us between the statuettes you gave

To Mom — two horses raised on hind legs, manes
Like banners in the wind — life just begun,
While hiding in the darkness of your face
Are lines that time will etch in years to come.

I hold the negative to light and find
The past's transparent shadows in my mind.

II) Habits

The house grows still and rhythms slowly fade,
The countless nights you stayed up late to paint
Then rose next day before the sun — habits
From childhood — fires to build; water to get;

A neighbor's farm to work, her house and barn
In silhouette against the day's first light
Along the road to school, that road that no
One uses any more. It was your way.

I sometimes I think I know what dreams had come
Those awful nights in hospital beds with wires
And tubes attached while all around you time,
Suspended in the rhythm of your heart,

Raged and we watched you try to rip away
Those years between that silhouette and you.

III) Everlast

I hear the *one two three* the *one two three*
These swift tight circles grow tighter as I
Move closer to the bag then back away.
The rhythm never varies. *One two three*

Mom warned my wife she'd have to leave the house,
Said she'd always had to leave herself.
The walls, the beams, the windows all became
Extensions of your pulsing one two three.

At least, she said, she knew you were alive.
One two one two one two I shift my feet,
Stand squarer to the bag. No circles now.
The fists strike the bag with a downward arc.

One two one two one two one two It stops.
The house grows still, and rhythms slowly fade.

henry 7. reneau, jr.

it's big & unplanned, full of tension & fear

the upside of anger
after the psychosis
of random pain
is deformity
suspended in time
like a blurred photograph
revealing itself
as an exposure of contempt
we become
an emotion taught to
loathe the alphabet
of recompense
in which
we only dismiss &
disparage
what we have
when we can't have what
we want

Mickey J. Corrigan

Private Room

Once, a man lay in a hospital bed
and no birds sang.

Once, a woman sat at the foot of the bed
and no dogs barked.

Once, the man's genes didn't have him up against a wall.
Night soothed.

Once, the woman was overfucked, not fucked over.
Sunlight dazzled.

Once, the man gave the woman a what for in a single malt diatribe.
Once, the man said he could make people dead and nobody laughed.
Once, the woman lived in a bus shelter and nobody cried.
Once, the man had a body like a cocked fist and no cats yowled.
Once, the woman took her punches with a smile and nobody died.
Once, the woman's smile looked like it was made with a can opener.

Once, the man loved the woman.
Birds sang. Dogs barked. Cats yowled.
Children cried.
Food tasted good. Everything tasted good.
Breezes cooled naked skin.
The weather was in a perfect mood.
The sky pearled. The globe twirled.
The sun kissed.

He insulated her bare wires.
She made his cells spark.

Nobody died.

Once, there was a difference between being something
and being something else.

Once upon a time in a hospital room
birds sang.

Nathalie Kuroiwa-Lewis

Awakenings

"Pick up the dog a-dings in yard.
It's been a week already," he tells me.
"And quit kettle whistling on stove.
Don't forget to scrub toilet
and make sure sink gleams like snow."

Yet, what I wish to tell him is thus:
that the day has just commenced
sun now rising-sphere of gold
knows my name and I am roused from deepest slumbers.
For so much time deep-earth diving
swimming in the vast reaches of the underworld only to find and
pluck crabs from underground caverns has left me weary and out of
oxygen.
Though I be appointed to search aerial jewels of fastidious Kings
Attempting someone else's stones in all corners of earth is precious
little for the heart's longings.

"The world is made for two-legged animals,"
he commands, finger pointed to the constellations.
"Hairy men with large breasts
Who build skyscrapers and fly winged machines in pale blue Who
run algorithms in their head and create computer chips deigned to
launch popping concoctions with sleight of finger on keyboard Who
conjure metadata tracking spells on SIM cards Who in riding wild
drones from remote controlled distances catch terror-fiends with
fire-breathing lassos Who in divining this and that, make treasures
that flood screens of e-portfolios and bounty faraway wells with
stygian elixirs."

Now it is my turn. So I tell him:
"But what of blue-haired sirens who redound ballads from the depths of the sea?
What of the gentle coos of babes that float like clouds in air?
Or better yet, the one that plays peek a boo beneath its mother's bosom?
What of the oracles of tea-induced hipsters who with eyes of aureole light sing tales of lost loves between gods and mortals?
What of the sweetest breath of children who flee trudgling devils with potions and rifles, seeking Gabriels at the gates of the borders?
What of the seraphic hands that splash golds and reds to design the "Panorama" seaport or those who breathe life to clay to conceive Copenhagen's apostles garbed in the flowing robes of yester years?
What of Nature's Wonders to be found when thunder like trains roar overhead through wide landscapes of skies, shaking earth below?
And what of She, Eurynome, the original maker, who first concocted Creation's Brew, far and wide?
What of Gaea who plotted the globe from North to South and East to West?
And what of that Maker who cast a David charming lips for worship and whose embrace you would never let go?"

"What of these?" I ask him
"Are they not made of the world too."
"Do they not count?"

My heart deluges the question so—
the stars above be bursting.

David Huntley

Warm Honey

Dropping shadows into a
Tripped up tide and fighting slowly,

It's like a web spun with dust
Throughout the night
To catch holes in the
Sky,

Puddles of ink
Paint the
Cobbles

But at night no one can see that,
Some notice
But not
Many,

The ones who do
Drink the warm honey of
Melancholy and rise higher
Than the first
Cloud of
Winter.

Malcolm Hassan

Textbook men

Some men have minds like
Boxes filled with
Textbooks, and
Stride as accurately
As meter wheels. Their
Perfectly formed sentences
Created by smooth even
Thoughts.
I look for a blast of freshness,
From a wave of cold water,
I search
The eyes for a flicker of
Vulnerability integral to the
Human condition.
I dig for the glimmer
That tells me I'm in the
Presence of a red-blooded
Creature: the stumbling
Of a word, a mistimed stride
A pair of socks splayed
Across a bedroom floor.
I'm hungry for a minor
Discrepancy: a
Dinner medal
Marking a perfectly ironed white shirt
A few dirty dishes
Sitting in a kitchen sink
...A single bone in a closet!
Proving that the past wasn't

Merely a perfectly designed vessel
Coasting over gently caressing
Waves.
Although
After all is said and done
All I find inside a perfectly
Clean house is a
Perfectly polished closet
Where seven identical unwrinkled
Shirts hang with pride.

Ross Knapp

Knifepoint

The menacing asshole has me at knifepoint.
He is easily the most terrifying person I've ever seen,
Sweaty palms holding the shard with an iron grip.
He looks dazed, delirious, deprived, drunk
Definitely depressed, desperate.
For some reason he has a horrible wide grin on his face
He darts around me, blocking off the only two doors to escape
I'm totally trapped now, there's no way out
His hair is disheveled and greasy like he hasn't showered in weeks
He has an awful unkempt beard
He's not too big and bulky, but definitely fit
Maybe I can take him
Eyes red and bloodshot like Lucifer himself
He cackles at me but is also curiously crying sometimes
He holds the massive steel blade a foot from my head like it's used to anoint
Of course it won't anoint, it will rip me to apart into a thousand shards of oblivion
It will be like I never existed at all
Like I was never born and lived and breathed
Like I never felt anything
Like I never thought anything
Like I never created anything
Like I never learned anything
Like I never helped anyone
Like I never accomplished anything
Like I never loved anyone
No, back to the abyss, the vast nothingness
You are a failure in everything you've ever done in your life anyway
You'd actually be helping everyone you care about
So just embrace the soothing darkness and nothingness
From dust to dust, ashes to ashes
Let him sink the blade into your flesh, over and over again,
So many times that your skin shines red with gushing gashes.

Don't resist him, give him whatever he wants and let him take you
Yes that's it, just put your arms down, we don't want a fight to ensue, you'd lose.
Maybe if you're lucky you'll get a good word in after all that volunteering and virtue!
But stop resisting! STOP IDIOT! Put your damn guard down!
Don't make him force you to jump in the lake and drown!
NO! The police! no nO NO! Hurry you COCKSUCKING FREAK drop your arms!
What the fuck are you waiting for?!
DO IT! NOW!!
No, you stupid crazy bitch
And I slowly lower the knife from being pointed straight at my chest to side
And start passing out of consciousness as I hear a slam and see a swarm of police

Jada Yee

Blackout

Terror can be fired from a flashlight;
a burning bullet that screams its way inside the cavities of curious eyes,
where fear takes possession with sharp calculation;
attaches to unsuspecting lungs to steal an irreplaceable breath.
It can drain the crystallized and clarified composure
from even the most eccentric phantom seeker.
Now, just a puppeteered victim with frightening symptoms,
living in a blackout, darker than indifference;
well-versed in silence, his name is long gone.

For the dilution of his dreams, he swallows insomnia.
Though his throat is calloused by the sharp edges, he thinks sedation is the answer.

Light is a noose; a noose awaiting surrender,
and he's fighting; he's fighting with all he has left.

How can they not understand that daylight is painful?
An underestimated truth, lingering with intentional spite.

He believes that he's fighting a terrifying fire;
a tortuous heat that, if given a chance,
would peel away his skin and confiscate his flesh.

Within this flammable contradiction, there's a voice; there's a face.
And it's been waiting to tell him he doesn't belong in this deepening grave.

If only he'd wander toward his own surviving whisper,
and allow it to soften the bright words he fears.

Luke Ritta

A table full of hope

The window shook from the howling wind outside the small cold attic.
Snow continued to pile high on the window ledge while a stray cat
screeched in the far distance.

Inside the bitterly cold attic an old peasant sat at a small wooden table.
On the table lay two objects, a spluttering candle that was letting off a acrid
smell and a clay bowl filled with warm pea soup.
The dying flame highlighted the
old peasants face, his grey beard was long and wiry and his skin was
covered in deep, dark winkles.

The peasant brought a spoonful of soup to his cracked lips and swallowed
the warm lumpy liquid, the flame from the candle swayed back and forward.

The amber glow was very weak now just like the heart of the old peasant.

Ingrid Calderon

my man blues

he likes the tang of copper wire
metallic tongue
against my mire
slap it up and swallow
carry me in your ribcage
I'll live there
and never tire
just grow and sprout right out your throat
make torrents there

include the necessary forevers
I'm those lax tones from groans and blood
from cell to lung
to fallen seed against my lips
all chewed to filth

it seems appropriate to confess
my simple sad
dull blade switch
comes up for air sometimes
when night skies open up
like half my body in and out your carriage
cold wind through toes encourage
warm face-down encounters
sliding eyes above high skies
spying down
come on inside
glide your tongue between hot whispers
like torrid gales
burning your open windows clean

New to Penny Ante Feud? Catch up on our back issues:

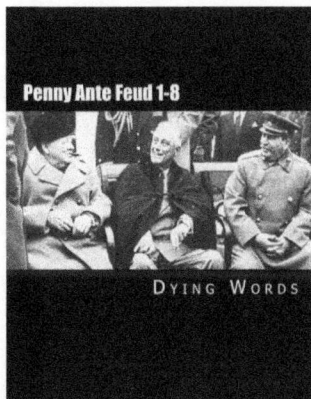

Penny Ante Feud 1-8 — DYING WORDS

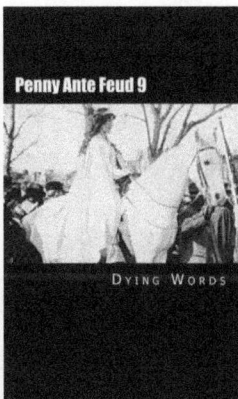

Penny Ante Feud 9 — DYING WORDS

Penny Ante Feud 10 — DYING WORDS

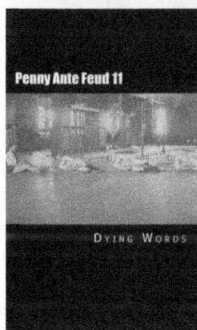

Penny Ante Feud 11 — DYING WORDS

Penny Ante Feud 12 — DYING WORDS

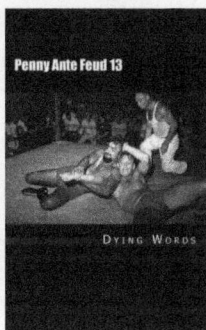

Penny Ante Feud 13 — DYING WORDS

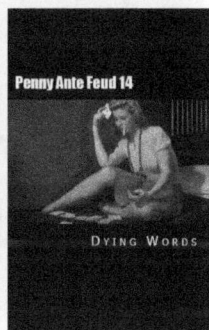

Penny Ante Feud 14 — DYING WORDS

Dying Words — Penny Ante Feud 15 — Walking the Dog Star

Please check our website
www.shoemusicpress.com for current pricing
(special bulk discount and author pricing
available).